# I SPY

## —— Animals In Art ——

*For My Family*

~

*FOREWORD*

A child looks at a painting and responds instinctively. As we grow up many of us forget how to do this. Our children can help us to remember how to see clearly, and we can encourage them never to lose confidence in their own judgement.

My own children helped me choose the pictures in this book and the animals to spy. I hope you will like them all, and that one day you may experience the thrill of seeing the original works of art and of discovering in them some familiar faces.

Lucy Micklethwait 1994

*Other titles in the series*
I Spy – An Alphabet In Art
I Spy – Numbers In Art
I Spy – Transport In Art

Cover picture: Edward Hicks, *Noah's Ark* (1846)
Title page picture: August Macke, *Landscape with Cows and Camel* (1914)

# I SPY

## Animals In Art

*Devised & selected by Lucy Micklethwait*

Collins
*An Imprint of HarperCollinsPublishers*

# I spy
## with my little eye

# a dog

Auguste Renoir, *The Luncheon of the Boating Party*

# I spy
# with my little eye

# a cat

Utagawa Hiroshige, *Asakusa Ricefields during the Cock Festival*

# I spy
## with my little eye

# a mouse

Jan van Os, *Fruit and Flowers in a Terracotta Vase*

# I spy
## with my little eye

# a rabbit

Titian, *The Virgin with the Rabbit*

# I spy
## with my little eye

# a horse

Fernand Léger, *The Great Parade*

# I spy
## with my little eye

# a squirrel

Hans Holbein the Younger, *A Lady with a Squirrel and a Starling*

# I spy
## with my little eye

# a lamb

Jan Steen, *The Poultry Yard*

# I spy
## with my little eye

# a brown
# cow

Peter Blume, *Winter, New Hampshire*

# I spy
## with my little eye

# a parrot

Lucas Cranach the Elder, *Cardinal Albrecht of Brandenburg as St. Jerome in his Study*

# I spy
## with my little eye

# a pig

Marc Chagall, *The Poet Reclining*

# I spy
## with my little eye

# a goat

François Boucher, *Spring*

# I spy
## with my little eye

# a tortoise

After Hieronymus Bosch, *The Concert in the Egg*

# I spy
# with my little eye

# a snake

Attributed to Isaac Oliver, *Rainbow Portrait of Queen Elizabeth I*

NON SINE SOLE
IRIS.

# I spy
## with my little eye

# a lion

Henri Rousseau, *Representatives of Foreign Powers Arriving to Hail the Republic as a Sign of Peace*

# I spy
## with my little eye

# a baby
# monkey

Indian, *Lady Holding Strings of Pearls*

# I spy
## with my little eye

# a crab

Pablo Picasso, *The Soles*

# I spy
## with my little eye

# an elephant

English, *The Animals, made on the Sixth Day of Creation*

# I spy
## with my little eye

# a camel

August Macke, *Landscape with Cows and Camel*

# I spy
## with my little eye

# a dragon

Bernardo Martorell, *St. George Slaying the Dragon*

# I spy
## with my little eye

# two tigers

*What do you spy?*

Edward Hicks, *Noah's Ark*

# — I Spied With My Little Eye —

## Dog
Auguste Renoir (1841-1919), *The Luncheon of the Boating Party* (1881)
The Phillips Collection, Washington, D.C.

## Cat
Utagawa Hiroshige (1797-1858), *Asakusa Ricefields during the Cock Festival* (1857) from the series *One Hundred Famous Views of Edo*
Fitzwilliam Museum, Cambridge

## Mouse
Jan van Os (1744-1808), *Fruit and Flowers in a Terracotta Vase* (1777-1778)
The National Gallery, London

## Rabbit
Titian (about 1488-1576), *The Virgin with the Rabbit* (1530)
Musée du Louvre, Paris

## Horse
Fernand Léger (1881-1955), *The Great Parade* (1954)
Solomon R. Guggenheim Museum, New York

## Squirrel
Hans Holbein the Younger (about 1497-1543), *A Lady with a Squirrel and a Starling* (about 1526-1528)
The National Gallery, London

## Lamb
Jan Steen (1626-1679), *The Poultry Yard* (1660)
Mauritshuis, The Hague

## Brown Cow
Peter Blume (1906-1992), *Winter, New Hampshire* (1927)
Museum of Fine Arts, Boston
Bequest of John T. Spaulding

# Parrot

Lucas Cranach the Elder (1472-1553), *Cardinal Albrecht of Brandenburg as St. Jerome in his Study* (1526)

The John and Mable Ringling Museum of Art, Sarasota, Florida

# Pig

Marc Chagall (1887-1985), *The Poet Reclining* (1915)

The Tate Gallery, London

# Goat

François Boucher (1703-1770), *Spring* from *The Four Seasons* (1755)

The Frick Collection, New York

# Tortoise

After Hieronymus Bosch (about 1450-1516), *The Concert in the Egg* (16th Century)

Musée des Beaux-Arts, Lille

# Snake

Attributed to Isaac Oliver (died 1617), *Rainbow Portrait of Queen Elizabeth I* (about 1600)

Hatfield House, Hertfordshire

# Lion

Henri Rousseau (1844-1910), *Representatives of Foreign Powers Arriving to Hail the Republic as a Sign of Peace* (1907)

Musée du Louvre, Paris
Picasso Bequest

# Baby Monkey

Indian, Mughal School, *Lady Holding Strings of Pearls* (about 1760)

The Victoria and Albert Museum, London

# Crab

Pablo Picasso (1881-1973), *The Soles* (1940)

Scottish National Gallery of Modern Art, Edinburgh

# Elephant

English manuscript, *The Animals, made on the Sixth Day of Creation*
from *The Ashmole Bestiary* (about 1210)
The Bodleian Library, Oxford

# Camel

August Macke (1887-1914), *Landscape with Cows and Camel* (1914)
Kunsthaus, Zürich

# Dragon

Bernardo Martorell (about 1400-1452), *St.George Slaying the Dragon*
(about 1438)
The Art Institute of Chicago
Gift of Mrs. Richard E. Danielson and Mrs. Chauncey McCormick

# Two Tigers

Edward Hicks (1780-1849), *Noah's Ark* (1846)
Philadelphia Museum of Art
Bequest of Lisa Norris Elkins

# ACKNOWLEDGEMENTS

The author and publishers would like to thank the galleries, museums, private collectors and copyright holders who have given their permission to reproduce the pictures in this book.

Utagawa Hiroshige, *Asakusa Ricefields during the Cock Festival*,
photograph © Fitzwilliam Museum, Cambridge
Jan van Os, *Fruit and Flowers in a Terracotta Vase*,
Hans Holbein the Younger, *A Lady with a Squirrel and a Starling*,
Reproduced by courtesy of the Trustees, The National Gallery, London
Titian, *The Virgin with the Rabbit,* Henri Rousseau, *Representatives of Foreign
Powers Arriving to Hail the Republic as a Sign of Peace*, photographs © R.M.N.
Fernand Léger, *The Great Parade*, © DACS 1994, photograph: David Heald
© The Solomon R. Guggenheim Foundation, New York
Jan Steen, *The Poultry Yard*, Inv. nr. 166 photograph © Foundation
Johan Maurits van Nassau, Mauritshuis, The Hague, Holland
Peter Blume, *Winter, New Hampshire*, © The Estate of Peter Blume/DACS, London/VAGA, New York 1994
Marc Chagall, *The Poet Reclining*, © ADAGP, Paris and DACS, London 1994
François Boucher, *Spring* from *The Four Seasons*, © The Frick Collection, New York
After Hieronymus Bosch, *The Concert in the Egg*, photograph: Giraudon/Bridgeman Art Library
Attributed to Isaac Oliver, *Rainbow Portrait of Queen Elizabeth I*, © Lord Salisbury
Indian painting, Mughal School, *Lady Holding Strings of Pearls*,
Courtesy of the Board of Trustees of the Victoria and Albert Museum
Pablo Picasso, *The Soles*, © DACS 1994
English manuscript, *The Animals, made on the Sixth Day of Creation*
from MS. Ashmole 1511, fol.6$^V$, The Bodleian Library, Oxford
Bernardo Martorell, Spanish (Catalonian), *St. George Slaying the Dragon*,
Photograph © 1993, The Art Institute of Chicago. All Rights Reserved.

First published in Great Britain by HarperCollins Ltd in 1994
Compilation and text © Lucy Micklethwait 1994

10 9 8 7 6

ISBN 0 00 193995 5 (HB)
ISBN 0 00 664407 4 (PB)